AF421848

Dedicated to Kim, Sam Re
"Omma"

김 삼 려
엄마

May 26, 1944-
January 25, 2024

Love, Insook

"Though the mountains be shaken and the hills removed, yet my unfailing love for you will not be shaken nor my covenant of peace be removed."
Isaiah 54:10

This book is dedicated to both my American family and my Korean family. You both will forever be in my heart.

Thank you to my translator friend, Yeonju Park, who has faithfully helped me over the last two decades, navigate both the language and culture of my birthplace.
You have been an incredible blessing to me!
If you'd like to read this book in hangeul, please see the last pages of this book, where Yeonju has translated this book in its entirety.

Also, thank you to InKAS in Korea, and KAAN (the Korean American Adoptee Adoptive Family Network.)
A portion of the proceeds of this book will be donated to help adoptees and their families through these organizations.

When I was ten months old,
I said goodbye to Korea.

I was too little to realize
where the plane was
taking me, but I could
already feel the love of
my adoptive parents.

Growing up in a military family, we lived in many places. First, we stayed in Japan. It was the land of cherry blossoms and kimonos, and a whole new language that I never got a chance to learn.

When I was three, California became my new home. I chased monarch butterflies, watched desert skies turn purple, and learned my new language. I soon forgot that the Korean word for butterfly was "nabi"(나비).

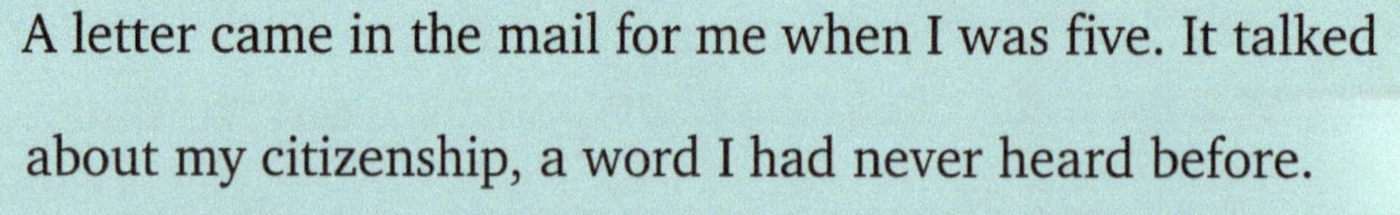

A letter came in the mail for me when I was five. It talked

about my citizenship, a word I had never heard before.

My Mom and Dad explained that I was adopted,

and I had just become an American citizen.

It was then that I noticed other people

asking my Mom, "Where is she from?"

My dark brown eyes and long black hair didn't look

the same as my Mom or my Dad's.

I asked my Mom, "Do I look like you?"

She wasn't quite sure what to say, so she

said yes. But when I looked in the mirror, I

could see differences.

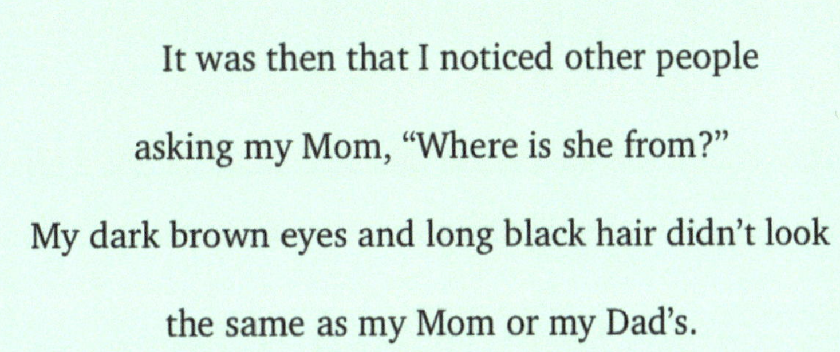

I loved my family, but I often wondered about my first family.
Did they think about me? Why was I given away? Do I look like
my Korean Mom or Dad? Do I have brothers or sisters?
It was like there was an empty picture frame, and I wanted to
fill it with photos of my life "before".

When I became a mom myself, it made my heart wonder even more.

Was she looking for me? Did she miss me?

I decided to contact an agency in Korea named InKAS. They helped adoptees find their birth parents. A lady named BongHee patiently walked me through the process of looking for my Mom. Eventually, she gave me the exciting news - they had found her!

I was amazed! I was also scared. What had her life been like while I had been apart from her? Would she want me in her life? Would I look like her?

When my sister started emailing pictures, I had no

doubt this was my family! I had an older brother

(oppa 오빠), two older sisters (unni 언니), and one

younger brother. They were so excited to get to

know me!

In the pictures, I looked the most like my mom (omma 엄마). Through the years, her prayers were for us to be reunited. In our first phone call, she said, "Hallelujah!" We both spoke it to each other, over and over. It was the one word that didn't need translating! After many more emails and phone calls, I decided to visit Korea. I had to meet my family.

I was saying hello to the country I had left behind. When I got off the plane, my older brother (oppa 오빠)was waiting for me.

He took me to meet my younger brother, one older sister (unni 언니), and my mom (omma 엄마).

When my mom (omma 엄마) turned to see me, tears that had been held for nearly thirty years fell. She opened her arms to me and pulled me close. I was the child she'd never truly let go.

My family shared stories.
Stories of losing my Dad ten years earlier. How they didn't name me for months, instead calling me "little one" (어린이). My father (appa 아빠) decided to name me Insook, (인숙) to match with my two older sisters, Minsook (민숙) and Changsook (창숙).

Over the next ten days of my visit, my family (kajok 가족) reintroduced me to Korea; to the food (bop 밥) and the hanboks (한복). We saw the beautiful mountains (san 산), trees (namoo 나무), and sea (pada 바다) together.

Ten days wasn't enough time to relive the last thirty years. But it was enough time to restore our family.

It's been nineteen years since I met my Korean family. My siblings have had more children, and so did I.

We kept in touch by emails, phone calls, and even visits. My mom (omma 엄마) met my American parents, and we all ate a meal together.

My life has changed so much, and I'm so thankful

that now my family includes loved ones in

both America (Migook 미국) and Korea (Hangook 한국).

It doesn't divide my love.

It makes me whole.

♡ Junghik, me, and Changsook

"Annyeong" means both hello and goodbye in Korean. I started my search to find my birth family when I was 25 years old. I had always wondered about who my first family was, and what was the story behind my adoption. I am forever grateful to KAAN (the Korean American Adoptee Adoptive Family Nework), for answering my email, and pointing me to an organization in Korea called InKAS. InKAS helped me not only in finding my birth mom (and two brothers and two sisters), but also provided me with translators who helped me with emails, as well as in person, when I traveled to Korea to meet my family for the first time.

Minook, Omma, me, Quincy, and Yeonju Park, our translator. :)

While in the middle of writing and illustrating this book, my Oppa called to tell me my Omma was dying. My return visit to Korea was hurried and unplanned, but it was still a beautiful time to spend with family, despite the reason. The mom that I had been separated from for most of my life, was able to hug and hold me tight as we said our final "annyeong."

My wish was for her to be able to hold this book in her hands, and relive the story with me. Even though that didn't happen, my original translator, Yeonju Park, was able to take the time and translate my book in Korea, so the rest of my family (and you as well!) could read it.

My little brother, my Omma, Quincy, and me!

My oppa, his daughter Soon Duck, her family, and my little brother Jungsik and his family.

Me and Omma! ♡

Eating fried ginseng!

Thank you (komopsumnida) for buying this book and supporting both my artistic endeavors and the adoption community. A portion of the proceeds of each book will go to KAAN, to help other adoptees and their families.

my adorable niece! ♡♡

Celebrating Chuseok!

안녕, 코리아
지은이 킴벌리 엘리스
I am forever grateful to Yeonju Park, for her amazing translation abilities,
her kind heart, and friendship through the years!

나는 10개월 아기였을 때 한국을 떠났어요. 그때 나는 너무 어려서 이 비행기가 나를 어디로 데려가는지 전혀 알 수 없었어요. 하지만 양부모님의 사랑은 이미 느낄 수 있었어요.

군인 가족으로 자라면서, 우리는 여러 곳에서 살았어요. 처음에 우린 일본에 살았어요. 그곳은 벗꽃과 기모노의 나라였고, 언어도 생소해서 나는 한번도 배워보지 못한 말이었어요.

세 살 때에 우리 새집은 캘리포니아가 되었어요. 나는 호랑나비를 쫓아 다니고, 사막의 하늘이 보라색으로 변해가는 것을 쳐다보고, 새로운 말을 배웠어요. 얼마 가지 않아 나는 나비를 한국어로 어떻게 말하는지 잊어버렸어요.

다섯 살이 되었을 때 나에 대한 메일이 한통 왔어요. 그 메일은 나의 시민권에 대해서 써졌어요. 시민권이라니, 한번도 들어보지 못한 단어였어요. 우리 엄마와 아빠는 내가 입양되었고, 이제 미국 시민이 된 것이라고 설명해주었어요. 그때서야 나는 사람들이 우리 엄마에게 "이 아이는 어디에서 온 거예요?"라고 묻는다는 것을 알아차렸어요. 나의 진한 갈색 눈동자와 검고 긴 머리칼이 엄마나 아빠와는 달랐던 거예요.

나는 엄마에게 물었어요, "나는 엄마를 닮았어요?" 엄마는 어떻게 말해줘야 할지 자신이 없었나 봐요. 그래서 그럼 이라고 말했어요. 하지만 거울을 보면, 나는 우리가 다른 것이 보였어요.

나는 우리 가족을 사랑해요. 하지만 나의 첫 번째 가족에 대해서 궁금해지기 시작했어요. 나에 대해서 생각할까? 나는 왜 여기로 보내졌을까? 나는 한국의 엄마나 아빠와 닮았을까? 나는 언니나 오빠, 동생이 있을까? 그건 마치 비어 있는 액자 같아서 나의 "예전" 이라는 사진을 채워 넣고 싶었어요. 다른 한국 사람들을 만났을 때, 그 사람들은 "Annyeonghaseyo?"(안녕하세요?)? 라고 말했는데, 나는 뭐라고 말할지, 어떻게 말해야 할지 몰랐어요.

내가 엄마가 되자 궁금함이 어느때 보다도 내 마음을 더 크게 채웠어요. 엄마는 나를 찾았을까? 나를 그리워했을까? 나는 InKAS라는 한국의 단체에 연락하기로 했어요. 그들은 입양인들이 친생 부모를 찾는 것을 도와줬어요. 봉희라는 이름의 해주었어요여자분은 인내심을 가지고 엄마를 찾는 과정에 나와 함께 . 마침내, 그녀는 나에게 아주 신나는 뉴스를 전해주었어요 – 그들이 엄마를 찾았답니다!

나는 아주 신났어요! 그리도 또 무섭기도 했어요. 내가 없었던 그 동안 그녀의 삶은 어떠했을까? 나를 다시 보고 싶어할까? 내가 그녀를 닮았을까?

나의 언니가 사진을 보내왔을 때, 이 사람들이 가족이라는 것을 믿을 수 밖에 없었어요! 나는 나보다 나이가 많은 남자형제 (오빠)와 두명의 여자형제 (언니), 그리고 남자 동생이 있었어요. 그들은 나를 알게 되어서 아주 기뻐했어요!

사진을 보면, 나는 나의 엄마 (Omma)를 가장 많이 닮았어요. 그 세월 동안, 그녀는 우리가 다시 만나게 해달라고 기도 했대요. 우리가 처음 전화 통화를 하게 되었을 때, 그녀는 "할렐루야"라고 외쳤어요. 우리는 그 말을 서로에게 몇 번이고 해주었어요. 그 말이 유일하게 우리 사이에 통역이 필요 없는 단어였어요.
이메일과 전화 통화가 여러 번 오고 간 후에, 나는 한국을 방문하기로 했어요. 가족을 만나야만 했어요.

내가 떠나왔던 나라에 안녕이라고 말했어요. 비행기에서 내렸을 때 오빠가 나를 기다리고 있었어요. 그는 나의 남동생과, 언니와 엄마를 소개해 주었어요.

엄마가 나를 돌아 볼 때, 거의 삼십 년을 참고 있던 눈물이 떨어졌어요. 나를 향해 두 팔을 벌리고 나를 꼭 끌어안아주었어요. 나는 엄마가 진정으로 한번도 보낸 적 없는 아이였어요.

가족들은 이야기를 들려줬어요. 10년 전 아빠는 돌아가셨다고 했어요. 몇 달이 지나도록 그들은 나를 이름으로 부르지 않았고, 대신 작은애라고 불렀어요.
나의 아빠는 나에게 인숙이라고 이름을 지어주었고, 그 이름은 다른 두명의 자매와 이름이 연결되는 거였어요, 민숙, 창숙 그리고 인숙.

내가 방문한 10일 동안, 나의 가족은 한국에 대해서 다시 소개해주었어요. 음식은 밥이었고, 옷은 한복이었어요. 우리는 아름다운 산을 보았고, 나무와 바다를 함께 보았어요.

10일은 지난 30년을 보상하기에는 너무 짧은 시간이었어요. 그러나 우리 가족을 다시 회복하기에는 충분했어요.

한국 가족을 만난지 이제 19년이 되어 가요. 나의 형제자매들도 아이들이 더 많아 졌고, 나도 그랬어요. 우리는 이메일로 계속 연락을 했고, 전화도 하고, 방문을 하기도 했어요. 나의 엄마는 우리 미국 부모님을 만났고, 모두 함께 식사를 했어요.

나에게 많은 것이 바뀌었어요. 내가 사랑하는 가족은 미국(아메리카)과 한국(코리아)에 모두 있다는 것이 너무 감사해요. 두 가족의 사랑이 나눠지는 게 아니예요. 그 둘이 나를 하나가 되게 해요.